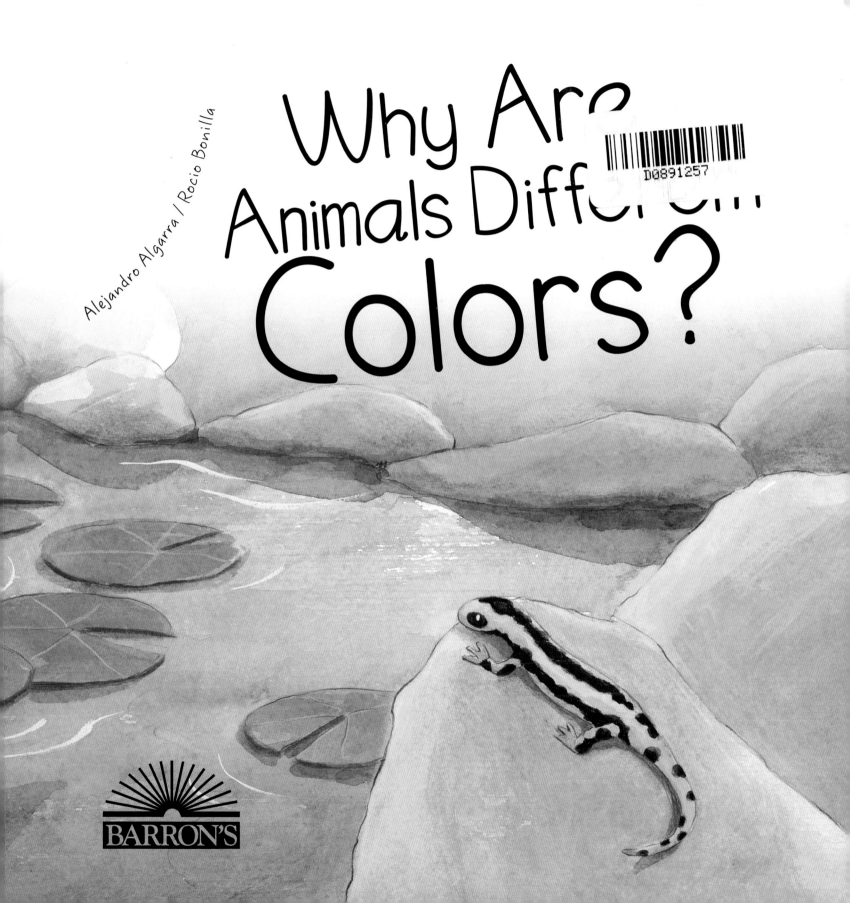

Why Are Animals Different Colors?

Alejandro Algarra / Rocio Bonilla

BARRON'S

2

Kate and Jack love animals. They are full of questions about why animals come in so many different colors!

"Hey, Jack, I wonder why some animals have such bright colors. And why do other animals have colors that make them blend into the background?" asks Kate. "And I really want to know why zebras have stripes!"

"I know!" replies Jack. "And I heard there are animals you can see through. Do you think it's true?"

"Let's find out!" shouts Kate.

Why are animals different colors?

Animals use colors for different reasons. Predators, or hunters, use color to get close to their prey (animals that are hunted by other animals for food). Prey use colors to hide from predators. The monarch butterfly uses bright colors to warn birds that they are poisonous and taste bad. Viceroy butterflies trick birds by "dressing up" as the monarch butterfly even though they are actually harmless.

Camouflage

Many animals use camouflage, or colors that help them blend in with their surroundings, so they can hide from predators. There are many examples of insects that do this. Moths have colors that blend in with tree bark so they can hide when they rest. Some caterpillars are able to use their shape and color to look just like the stem of a plant!

Hiding hunters

Some predators use camouflage so their prey does not see them coming! For example, the tiger's fur is yellow with black stripes. These colors make the tiger almost invisible when it hunts in its environment, where it easily blends in with tall, yellow grass. Be careful! Hunters can hide, too!

Changing colors

The kings of camouflage in the animal world are those that can change color to match the color of their surroundings. On land, the most famous example is the chameleon. Chameleons change colors not only to become invisible but also to show their moods to fellow chameleons. They can even change color to show if they are healthy or sick. Do you think the colorful chameleon is happy?

10

Underwater camouflage

Many animals in the ocean can also change colors.
Some fish can become lighter or darker depending
on the time of day or night. The sole is a master of
camouflage! When it lies flat on the sand it is almost
impossible to see because it matches the background
colors perfectly.

Cuttlefish colors

In the sea, octopuses, squid, and especially cuttlefish make the most amazing color changes. These intelligent animals can change their colors to communicate with one another, to scare off predators, to camouflage themselves, or to look like a different animal or fish. If that's not enough, they can also change the designs on their skin!

Warning colors

Some animals do not use colors to hide. They use bright colors to warn other animals that they are dangerous. The most common warning colors are combinations of white, black, yellow, and red. Some frogs and salamanders display these colors, as do some snakes and lizards, many insects, and spiders.

Don't touch me! Don't eat me!

The orange and black found on some butterflies warns that they don't taste good. Wasps have black and yellow stripes to warn that they sting. That way, birds do not eat them. The skunk, which has a white stripe over a black background down its back and tail, says "Don't bother me! Don't come near me or I'll spray you with a very stinky liquid!" Thank goodness they warn us!

Tricky disguises

Warning colors are so helpful that some snakes use them to protect themselves. One of the most poisonous snakes in America is the coral snake. It shows that it is poisonous with the yellow, black, and red stripes that run the entire length of its body. Other snakes that are totally harmless, like the scarlet king snake, use a striped design that is similar to that of the coral snake to trick any animal that wants to eat it. Pretty smart! Can you guess which of these snakes is the coral and which is the scarlet king?

Is it a wasp or a fly?

If you walk through a garden or a meadow, it might be easy to spot insects that copy the warning colors of other insects. You might see some insects that look like wasps flying among the flowers, but if you look up close you will see that they are actually hoverflies! Hoverflies are totally harmless but are very good at disguising themselves. Some of them imitate wasps, while others disguise themselves as bees. Don't let them fool you!

Sneaky eyes

Some animals trick predators by scaring them with flashes of color, or false eyes, called eyespots. Many butterflies have two large eyespots on the inside of their wings. Just in case the camouflage colors on the outside of their wings do not work, the butterfly will suddenly open its wings and show its eyespots. With luck, the predator will be frightened for an instant, and the butterfly will have enough time to get away.

Colors of love

Many animals—especially birds—use colors to attract a mate. The male peacock has an amazing train of feathers near its tail that is full of beautiful colors: green, blue, gold . . . all of it sparkling! The female, however, has dull colors that are perfect for hiding behind plants and grass. The male competes with other males to show off the most magnificent train, and the female chooses the winner, who will become the father of her babies.

Colors to find customers

Cleaner fish have a dark-colored stripe that runs along the length of their body from head to tail. With this design, they show who they are to the other fish. Large and small fish come to them to be cleaned. As the cleaner works on one of them, the others patiently await their turn. In this way, they all win: The cleaner eats, and the other fish leave with their bodies clean of dead skin and parasites, or smaller creatures that live on and feed on larger creatures.

The zebra's stripes

Zebras look like horses wearing striped pajamas! But, what are those stripes for? Some scientists think that the stripes protect zebras from predators, such as lions and hyenas. If you look at a herd of zebras from far away, it's hard to tell where one zebra ends and another begins. And, when they start running, the motion of all those stripes confuses the hunter. The hunter pauses, and the zebras—with some luck—have enough time to escape.

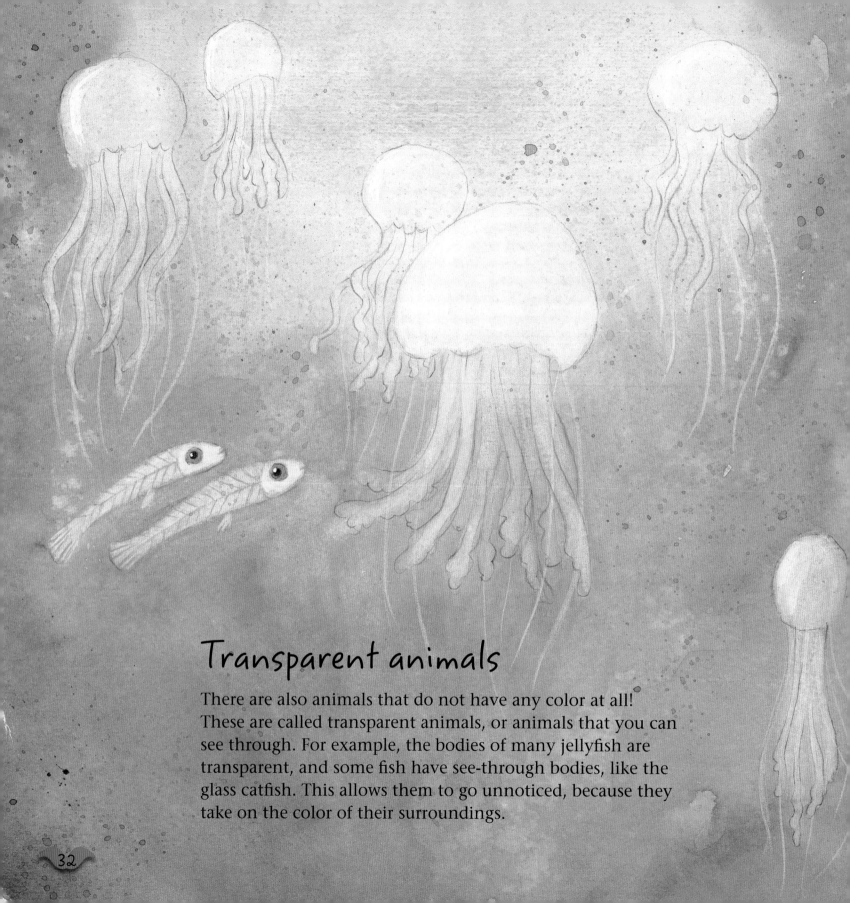

Transparent animals

There are also animals that do not have any color at all! These are called transparent animals, or animals that you can see through. For example, the bodies of many jellyfish are transparent, and some fish have see-through bodies, like the glass catfish. This allows them to go unnoticed, because they take on the color of their surroundings.

"Wow, animals use color in such cool ways!" says Kate.

"I'm really glad we looked it up!" adds Jack. "Let's go play hide and seek!"

"You'll never blend into your surroundings with that striped shirt!" laughs Kate.

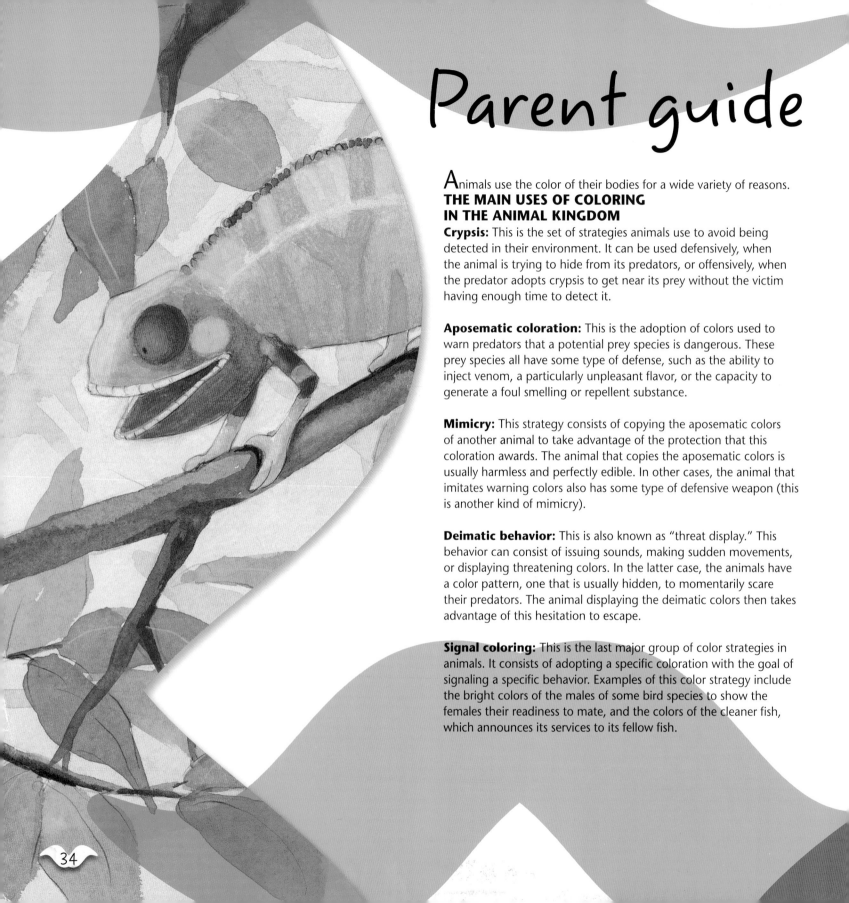

Parent guide

Animals use the color of their bodies for a wide variety of reasons.

THE MAIN USES OF COLORING IN THE ANIMAL KINGDOM

Crypsis: This is the set of strategies animals use to avoid being detected in their environment. It can be used defensively, when the animal is trying to hide from its predators, or offensively, when the predator adopts crypsis to get near its prey without the victim having enough time to detect it.

Aposematic coloration: This is the adoption of colors used to warn predators that a potential prey species is dangerous. These prey species all have some type of defense, such as the ability to inject venom, a particularly unpleasant flavor, or the capacity to generate a foul smelling or repellent substance.

Mimicry: This strategy consists of copying the aposematic colors of another animal to take advantage of the protection that this coloration awards. The animal that copies the aposematic colors is usually harmless and perfectly edible. In other cases, the animal that imitates warning colors also has some type of defensive weapon (this is another kind of mimicry).

Deimatic behavior: This is also known as "threat display." This behavior can consist of issuing sounds, making sudden movements, or displaying threatening colors. In the latter case, the animals have a color pattern, one that is usually hidden, to momentarily scare their predators. The animal displaying the deimatic colors then takes advantage of this hesitation to escape.

Signal coloring: This is the last major group of color strategies in animals. It consists of adopting a specific coloration with the goal of signaling a specific behavior. Examples of this color strategy include the bright colors of the males of some bird species to show the females their readiness to mate, and the colors of the cleaner fish, which announces its services to its fellow fish.

THE WAY ANIMALS PRODUCE COLOR

Color production varies according to the species and the group to which they belong. Some animals produce pigments in their skin that gives them color. These pigments include melanin. In other cases, their color is not due to a pigment but to the effect caused by the light reflecting off of microscopic structures on the body. One example of this is the feathers of the male peacock (as well as the iridescent colors of the feathers of many birds).

When viewed under a microscope, these feathers reveal that they are actually a single color, usually brownish. The effects of the incredible colors of these feathers are due to the way in which the light reflects off of them. Some animals are capable of changing colors thanks to the fact that their skin has specialized cells that concentrate or disperse the pigment inside them. The typical example among vertebrates is the chameleon, while among invertebrates they are the cuttlefish and the octopus. The animals that can change colors can use this ability for a variety of purposes: as a means of crypsis to blend in with their surroundings; to communicate with the fellow members of their species, including sexual behavior; to adopt warning colors, such as a very poisonous octopus species that lives in the waters of the Pacific Ocean; to make threatening displays, or deimatic displays; and as an expression of their state of health.

Disruptive coloring: This is one of the most effective ways of getting cryptic coloring. It consists of displaying patterns that seem extremely striking when isolated from the environment, but when seen in nature manage to perfectly camouflage the animal that adopts this coloring. Disruptive colors produce the effect of breaking up the visible silhouette of an animal so that it blends in with its surroundings. Military camouflage colors are based on the disruptive coloring in the animal world.

Countershading: This is a kind of coloring used by a large number of animals from all groups to blend in with their surroundings. Thanks to countershading, they manage to practically eliminate their shadow, which makes them virtually disappear. In land-dwelling animals, this is achieved with more pronounced colors on the back and lighter or almost white colors on the belly. Think about deer, for example, or squirrels. Their countershaded coloring makes them almost invisible in their habitat when we see them from the side. Countershading is also common in birds. In the ocean, countershading works in a different way: The backs or upper sides of fish (including sharks), marine mammals, and birds like penguins is often a very dark color, while their bellies and lower parts are very light or white. In this way, if we look at these animals inside the water from above, their dark color blends in with the rest of the water, which is usually dark. But, if we see these animals swimming above us, the white color of their bellies makes them blend in with the light provided by the sunlight that filters in through the water toward the sea floor. This strategy is effective for hiding both from hunters and from possible prey, which might be hunted by predator animals such as sharks.

Seasonal variation: Some animals change the color of their fur or feathers depending on the season of the year. This happens in predators like the arctic fox, whose brown or grayish fur becomes white during the winter months, when their surroundings are blanketed in snow. It also happens in non-predators like the arctic hare and the ptarmigan, which "dress up" in white during the winter to better hide from their enemies.

First edition for the United States and Canada published in 2016 by Barron's Educational Series, Inc.

© Gemser Publications, S.L. 2015
El Castell, 38 08329 Teiá (Barcelona, Spain)
www.mercedesros.com

Text: Alejandro Algarra
Design and layout: Estudi Guasch, S.L.
Illustration: Rocio Bonilla

All inquiries should be addressed to:
Barron's Educational Series, Inc.
250 Wireless Boulevard
Hauppauge, NY 11788
www.barronseduc.com

ISBN: 978-1-4380-0893-6

Library of Congress Control No.: 2016930609

Date of Manufacture: April 2016
Manufactured by: L. Rex Printing Company Limited, Dongguan City, Guangdong, China

Printed in China
9 8 7 6 5 4 3 2 1